God's
DAILY
ANSWER

devotions to renew your soul

FOR MEN

God's
DAILY
ANSWER

devotions to renew your soul

FOR MEN

God is inscrutable—there will always be aspects of His person that we aren't capable of understanding. But He knows our need for answers and has responded by giving us the Scriptures, rich oral traditions, and the witness of our hearts to let us know what we can expect from Him, how He wishes to interact with us, and the various aspects of His character. He encourages us to ask, seek, and find.

If you have questions about God and what He expects from you, *God's Daily Answer for Men* was designed for you. As you read, you will hear what God has to say about the issues you are facing in the course of your everyday life—topics like decisions, finances, integrity, work, and success. We hope you will also come to know more intimately the One who holds *all* the answers—the One who holds you in the palm of His hand.

TABLE OF CONTENTS

The best treasure
that a man can attain unto in this world
is true knowledge;
even the knowledge of himself.

—

JACOB BOEHME

SATISFACTION

He shall see the labor of His soul, and be satisfied.
ISAIAH 53:11

There's nothing quite like putting your all into a project—whether at home or at work—knowing you've done your best, then seeing it turn out right. You get a huge sense of satisfaction from a job well done.

Whether you're building a birdhouse or laboring under the hood of your car, when the job is complete, this feeling of satisfaction wells up inside you. Is that pride? It can be if you start boasting about it. But satisfaction is a God-given emotion: you know your hard work has paid off.

Savor the moment. Life is full of many frustrations and long-term, loose-ended projects, so enjoy each chunk of satisfaction and accomplishment that comes your way.

Look at a day when you are supremely satisfied at the end. It's not a day when you lounge around doing nothing. It's when you've had everything to do, and you've done it.

MARGARET THATCHER

The happy people are those who
are producing something.

WILLIAM RALPH INGE

There is no happiness except in the realization
that we have accomplished something.

HENRY FORD

He is rich that is satisfied.

THOMAS FULLER

Well-spoken words bring satisfaction;
well-done work has its own reward.

PROVERBS 12:14 THE MESSAGE

IDENTITY

You shaped me first inside, then out;
you formed me in my mother's womb. ...
Body and soul, I am marvelously made!

PSALM 139:13–14 THE MESSAGE

God loves you and is intimately concerned with your life, to the point that "the very hairs of your head are all numbered" (Matt. 10:30). And He was just as involved right from the beginning with the creation of your spirit, soul, and body.

Who you are is largely determined by your inherited genetic traits and your upbringing, but there is more to you than just that. Spirit, soul, and body, you are a unique creation of God—a man who is known by Him and loved by Him. He designed you the way you are for a reason.

There's always room to improve your character and overcome weaknesses, but it's important to accept and love yourself as the unique person God created you to be.

He who counts the stars and calls them
by their names is in no danger of forgetting
His own children.

CHARLES HADDON SPURGEON

The way in which we think of ourselves has everything to do with how our world sees us.

ARLENE RAVEN

Is it a small thing in your eyes to be loved by God—to be the son, the spouse, the love, the delight of the King of glory?

RICHARD BAXTER

Everything is good when it leaves the Creator's hands.

JEAN-JACQUES ROUSSEAU

Your hands have made me and fashioned me.

JOB 10:8

WEALTH

It is God who gives you power to get wealth.
DEUTERONOMY 8:18

If you're struggling financially, you may wish that you were wealthy, but more money may not be the answer. No matter what your financial status, a few basic principles should be at work in your life.

First, you need to trust God, the ultimate Source of all blessings. Then, consider this: what good is wealth without contentment—the ability to enjoy what you have without always striving for more? And last, but not least, you should be practicing wise financial management.

Above all, remember life is much more than money and the things money can buy. Wealth is fine if you have it, but most valuable in life are those things that money can't buy.

The real measure of our wealth is how much we'd be worth if we lost all our money.
JOHN HENRY JOWETT

God only and not wealth, maintains the world.

MARTIN LUTHER

If you want to feel rich, just count all the things
you have that money can't buy.

AUTHOR UNKNOWN

There is nothing wrong with people
possessing riches. The wrong comes
when riches possess people.

BILLY GRAHAM

Command those who are rich in this present age
not to ... trust in uncertain riches but in
the living God, who gives us richly all things to enjoy.

1 TIMOTHY 6:17

JUSTICE

Defend the poor and fatherless;
do justice to the afflicted and needy.

PSALM 82:3

When you see a coworker being harassed or taken advantage of, and you speak up about it, you're striving for what's right and just. When a con artist defrauds an elderly lady of her life savings and you call the authorities, it's justice you're seeking.

God is a God of justice. He doesn't turn a blind eye to injustice, and He doesn't want you to. Speaking up or doing something when you see wrong being done is a God-given instinct. Just be sure that it's justice you seek and not "an-eye-for-an-eye" revenge.

Once you've done what you can, leave matters in the hands of those in authority. And most importantly, always leave them in the hands of God.

If it is thought that justice is with us,
it will give birth to courage.

ELMER DAVIS

The pearl of justice is found in
the heart of mercy.

SAINT CATHERINE OF SIENA

No human actions ever were intended by
the Maker of men to be guided by balances
of expediency, but by balances of justice.

JOHN RUSKIN

Justice and power must be brought together,
so that whatever is just may be powerful,
and whatever is powerful may be just.

BLAISE PASCAL

He hath shewed thee, O man, what is good;
and what doth the LORD require of thee,
but to do justly, and to love mercy.

MICAH 8:6 KJV

SCRIPTURE

Every part of Scripture is God-breathed and useful
one way or another—showing us truth …
correcting our mistakes, training us to live God's way.
2 TIMOTHY 3:16 THE MESSAGE

When you come face-to-face with a dilemma—a fad comes home with your children, or the media confronts you with a new worldview, for example—you need to know what's right and wrong, what's acceptable and what is not. You need an authoritative standard by which to measure the issues of life.

The Bible is the ultimate word on what God has determined is truth or error, morally right or wrong. Just as the National Bureau of Standards in Washington, D.C., sets the mark for weights, measurement, time, and mass, so you have a spiritual Bureau of Standards—the Bible.

Everything that comes into your life must be placed alongside the Scriptures to see how it measures up.

The Bible is God's chart for you to steer by,
to keep you from the bottom of the sea, and
to show you where the harbor is, and how to
reach it without running on rocks and bars.
HENRY WARD BEECHER

The Bible was given to bear witness to one God,
Creator and Sustainer of the universe, through
Christ, Redeemer of sinful man. It presents
one continuous story—that of human redemption.

M. F. UNGER

God did not write a book and send it by
messenger to be read at a distance by unaided
minds. He spoke a Book and lives in His spoken
words, constantly speaking His words and causing
the power of them to persist across the years.

A. W. TOZER

When you have read the Bible, you will know it
is the word of God, because you will have found it
the key to your own heart, your own
happiness and your duty.

WOODROW WILSON

To the law and to the testimony!
If they do not speak according to this word,
it is because there is no light in them.

ISAIAH 8:20

THOUGHTS

Whatever things are true, whatever things are noble, whatever things are just, whatever things are pure ... meditate on these things.

PHILIPPIANS 4:8

God has given human beings amazing minds. Scientists are still trying to figure out how the whole process of thinking works. The ability to envision things, dream up new concepts, work out problems, and make choices, is a gift of God.

Your thoughts are not mere nothings; they are vitally important. Every single deed begins with a thought. Even thoughts that don't lead to action color your attitude either positively or negatively, and affect your entire outlook—which in turn affects you and others around you.

Dwelling on negative thoughts will drag you down; but the good news is that if you make a habit of choosing to think encouraging, positive, caring thoughts, they will eventually make your whole world better!

Keep your thoughts right, for as you think,
so are you.

HENRY H. BUCKLEY

Think positively and masterfully, with confidence
and faith, and life becomes more secure,
more fraught with action, richer in
achievement and experience.

EDDIE RICKENBACKER

Our best friends and our worst enemies are
our thoughts. A thought can do us more good
than a doctor or a banker or a faithful friend.
It can also do us more harm than a brick.

FRANK CRANE

It concerns us to keep a strict guard
upon our thoughts, because God
takes particular notice of them.

MATTHEW HENRY

As he thinks in his heart, so is he.

PROVERBS 23:7

SPEECH

Gracious speech is like clover honey—
good taste to the soul, quick energy for the body.

PROVERBS 16:24 THE MESSAGE

If you were to always blurt out what was on your mind without considering how it would affect others, you'd learn that words have the power to discourage. Your words also have great power to *encourage* when you take the time to speak kindly, point out a fault gently, or share an inspiring insight.

Encouraging words can breathe life into people who have all but given up. You don't need to be a great motivational speaker; you just need to speak from your heart and ask yourself, "What can I say that would help this person?"

This doesn't mean you need to walk on eggshells around people and not speak the truth. You must speak the truth, but as Ephesians 4:15 says, do it in a loving manner.

Speaking without thinking is shooting
without aiming.

SIR WILLIAM GURNEY BENHAM

Kind words produce their image on men's souls,
and a beautiful image it is. They smooth,
and quiet, and comfort the hearer.

BLAISE PASCAL

Good words are worth much, and cost little.

GEORGE HERBERT

Little keys can open big locks.
Simple words can express great thoughts.

WILLIAM ARTHUR WARD

Choose your words carefully and be ready
to give answers to anyone who asks questions.

COLOSSIANS 4:6 CEV

PATIENCE

*Better a patient man than a warrior, a man who
controls his temper than one who takes a city.*

You've probably seen some examples of angry
impatience—a fellow worker cursing and
throwing tools around, or a driver fuming when he
or she has to wait an extra thirty seconds in traffic.
But all of us need to learn more patience.

Being patient doesn't mean standing around
all day. You were designed to be active, to think up
solutions, to do your best to make things happen.
But some things take time no matter how hard you
push, so pace yourself, relax.

Trusting God is a large part of being patient.
You have to trust God is going to make things work
out. You have to trust that given time, wisdom, and
direction, a solution will be found. So have faith.
Have patience.

Patience is bitter, but its fruit is sweet.

JEAN-JACQUES ROUSSEAU

Be patient toward all that is unsolved
in your heart.

DAG HAMMARSKJÖLD

Teach us, O Lord, the disciplines of patience,
for to wait is often harder than to work.

PETER MARSHALL

Be patient with everyone, but above all,
with yourself.

SAINT FRANCIS DE SALES

Farmers do this all the time, waiting for their
valuable crops to mature, patiently letting the rain
do its slow but sure work. Be patient like that.

JAMES 5:7 THE MESSAGE

LOVE

*Jesus said, "These things I command you,
that you love one another."*

JOHN 15:17

God's Word contains a number of commandments, and you'll be a better man for obeying them. The commands repeated most often in the New Testament are to love God and to love others.

The Bible says *the* overriding rule of life is to love! It is to be the underlying motive for everything you do. Yet it's so easy to get distracted doing even good things. You can get so caught up in doing things for your family, for instance, that you forget to do them with a loving attitude.

It's not always easy to make sure everything you do is motivated by Christ's love, so pray and ask God to help you. He will honor that prayer. Remember, God doesn't expect perfection. But He does expect you to love.

Love is the only spiritual power that can overcome
the self-centeredness that is inherent
in being alive.

ARNOLD JOSEPH TOYNBEE

I have found the paradox that if I love until
it hurts, then there is no hurt,
but only more love.

SAINT TERESA

He who is filled with love is filled
with God himself.

SAINT AUGUSTINE OF HIPPO

Love seeks one thing only:
the good of the one loved.

THOMAS MERTON

Christ's love ... has the first and last word
in everything we do.
2 CORINTHIANS 5:14 THE MESSAGE

WORK

*Serve wholeheartedly, as if you were serving the Lord,
not men, because you know that the Lord will reward
everyone for whatever good he does.*

EPHESIANS 6:7–8 NIV

If you love what you do, it's easy to put your
heart into it and make sure you consistently
deliver quality work. But there are times when even
work you enjoy becomes just that—plain hard work.
A piece keeps coming back for revisions. Unexpected
problems arise. Snags happen. Delays. Pleasure turns
into frustration.

Or you may be a person who—because of
circumstances you can't control—must work at a
job you dislike. *Then* what motivates you to do your
best? Commit your work to God. Do your very best
for Him. In that way, you'll be doing a service for
yourself as well. You simply cannot lose when you
set out to please God.

Work becomes worship when done for the Lord.

AUTHOR UNKNOWN

He who labors as he prays lifts up his heart
to God with his hands.

SAINT BERNARD OF CLAIRVAUX

Hard work is a thrill and joy when you are
in the will of God.

ROBERT A. COOK

Honest labor bears a lovely face.

THOMAS DEKKER

Do you see a man who excels in his work?
He will stand before kings; he will not
stand before unknown men.

PROVERBS 22:29

KINDNESS

*Jesus said, "Invite the poor, the crippled, the lame,
and the blind. Then at the resurrection of
the godly, God will reward you for inviting
those who can't repay you."*

LUKE 14:13–14 TLB

You can get real pleasure from doing kind things for your wife, your children, and your friends—helping them when they need help, taking the time to listen, or getting a gift that shows them you care. But did you know that showing kindness to those outside your circle can bring joy as well?

The Bible says that when you are kind to those who are unable to do anything for you in return, you will be rewarded by God. That's the warm sense of satisfaction you feel when you reach out with kindness to someone who needs your help. It's like God pays you back when the person in question cannot. So reach out whenever you can, and feel the touch of God's hand on your life.

True charity is the desire to be useful to others
without thought of recompense.

EMANUEL SWEDENBORG

Constant kindness can accomplish much.
As the sun makes ice melt, kindness causes
misunderstanding, mistrust and hostility
to evaporate.

ALBERT SCHWEITZER

Be the living expression of God's kindness:
kindness in your face, kindness in your eyes,
kindness in your smile,
kindness in your warm greeting.

MOTHER TERESA

Be kind. Remember that everyone you meet
is fighting a hard battle.

HARRY THOMPSON

Be kindly affectionate to one another
with brotherly love, in honor giving
preference to one another.

ROMANS 12:10

PRAYER

Pray without ceasing.

1 THESSALONIANS 5:17

If you get up early every morning to spend time praying, that's wonderful! But it could be that finding time in your busy schedule for prayer is a real challenge.

The good news is you can pray *all* the time, *wherever* you are, *whatever* you're doing. Remember, prayer simply means talking to God, person to person, friend to friend. He may be the all-powerful Creator of the universe, but He always has time for you. So talk to Him throughout your day. Talk to Him about everything.

You can praise God for His wonders, you can pray for wisdom, you can ask Him to resolve a problem, you can thank Him for what He's already done—and you can do it all day long.

Never wait for fitter time or place to talk to him. To wait till you go to church or to your room is to make him wait. He will listen as you walk.

GEORGE MACDONALD

We should speak to God from our own hearts
and talk to him as a child talks to his father.

CHARLES HADDON SPURGEON

Prayer is conversation with God.

CLEMENT OF ALEXANDRIA

When you can't put your prayers into words,
God hears your heart.

AUTHOR UNKNOWN

Instead of worrying, pray. Let petitions and praises
shape your worries into prayers,
letting God know your concerns.

PHILIPPIANS 4:6 THE MESSAGE

LIFE

*I've decided that there's nothing better to do
than go ahead and have a good time
and get the most we can out of life.*

ECCLESIASTES 3:9 THE MESSAGE

You've heard the expression "That's just the way life is." It sounds like an injustice that has to be endured. Or you've heard, "Life is beautiful," and you wonder if the speaker ever held a nine-to-five job, paid bills, or took care of a wife and kids. The truth: that life consists of all of these things and much more.

God has given you life, but He hasn't left you to navigate through all of its wonders, difficulties, hard work, and happiness on your own. He has also given you clear instructions on how to live. The Bible is your handbook. Follow its commandments and principles, and you'll get the most out of every day in this life and the next.

Life is far more than pleasures, possessions, or plaques on the wall. Life, in all its many facets, is a gift from God every day.

The value of life lies not in the length of days,
but in the use we make of them.

MICHEL DE MONTAIGNE

Let God have your life; he can do more
with it than you can.

DWIGHT L. MOODY

I will not just live my life. I will not
just spend my life. I will invest my life.

HELEN KELLER

Life is a great big canvas;
throw all the paint on it you can.

DANNY KAYE

Jesus said, "One's life does not consist
in the abundance of the things he possesses."

LUKE 12:15

HONESTY

Speak each man the truth to his neighbor.

ZECHARIAH 8:16

You know that telling the truth in a court of law is important. But what about day-to-day life where you're not "under oath"? Many people feel it's acceptable to mislead others or outright lie in daily life. To them it's a matter of convenience to avoid confrontations and consequences. But that doesn't make it right.

God wants you to be honest with others and with yourself—without exception, without hesitation. Do so and you'll have a reputation for honesty. You will soon gain the respect of those around you. Best of all, you'll have the satisfaction of knowing you're living a life that honors God.

Honesty has a beautiful and refreshing simplicity about it. No ulterior motives. No hidden meanings.

CHARLES R. SWINDOLL

To be honest as this world goes,
is to be one man picked out of a thousand.

WILLIAM SHAKESPEARE

Honesty consists of the unwillingness to lie to
others; maturity, which is equally hard to attain,
consists of the unwillingness to lie to oneself.

SYDNEY J. HARRIS

I consider the most enviable of all titles,
the character of an honest man.

GEORGE WASHINGTON

Do not lie. Do not deceive one another.

LEVITICUS 19:11 NIV

PERSEVERANCE

Perseverance must finish its work so that you may be mature and complete, not lacking anything.

JAMES 1:4 NIV

Perseverance means keeping at something and refusing to quit till it's done. It isn't a problem when you're doing something you enjoy. Every hour you work on your hobby is a pleasure, whether restoring a vintage auto, gardening, or whatever your passion.

Where you need perseverance is when you're working on an unpleasant, long-term project. It requires self-discipline to diligently work at it every day without procrastinating.

How do you motivate yourself? Pray for God's inspiration; take breaks; track your progress; joke about it; play music; get help; think about how you'll spend the money or enjoy the reward it will yield. Remind yourself *why* you're doing it. And remember: this, too, shall pass.

Great works are performed, not by strength,
but by perseverance.

SAMUEL JOHNSON

Permanence, perseverance, and persistence
in spite of all obstacles, discouragements,
and impossibilities: It is this, that in all things
distinguishes the strong soul from the weak.

SIR FRANCIS DRAKE

Energy and persistence conquer all things.

BENJAMIN FRANKLIN

There must be a beginning to any great matter,
but the continuing to the end until it
be thoroughly finished yields the true glory.

THOMAS CARLYLE

Water wears away stones.

JOB 14:19 NIV

MERCY

Jesus said, "Blessed are the merciful,
for they shall obtain mercy."

MATTHEW 5:7

When Jesus said to be merciful, He was aware there needed to be retribution for breaking rules. Jesus knew all about repeat offenders. He knew about "tough love" two thousand years before the term was coined.

Still, he exhorts you to be merciful. There are enough times when you need to enforce rules and let people feel the full consequences for their actions. But in the midst of justice, there are times when mercy is more effective.

King David asked, "If you, GOD, kept records on wrongdoings, who would stand a chance? As it turns out, forgiveness is your habit" (Ps. 130:3 THE MESSAGE). Follow God's example and make a habit of being merciful.

He who demands mercy and shows none ruins the bridge over which he himself is to pass.

THOMAS ADAMS

Mercy is compassion in action.

AUTHOR UNKNOWN

Nothing graces the Christian soul
as much as mercy.

SAINT AMBROSE

Two works of mercy set a man free: forgive
and you will be forgiven,
and give and you will receive.

SAINT AUGUSTINE OF HIPPO

*Jesus said, "Be merciful,
just as your Father is merciful."*

LUKE 6:36 NIV

PROTECTION

*God's angel sets up a circle of protection
around us while we pray.*

PSALM 34:7 THE MESSAGE

Some people believe everything happens for
a reason. Others think life simply happens
and God's children are touched with pain and
accidents like everyone else. Who's right? It's a
question that may not be answered in this life.

What you can be sure of is God has the *power*
to protect you and He has *promised* to do so. When
you pray, He can do the miraculous to keep you safe.
And yet, bad things do happen to good people. It is
best to remember that even when you find yourself
passing through the valley of the shadow of death,
God will be with you. He will walk every inch of
that valley with you. And together you will reach
the other side.

Those who walk in God's shadow
are not threatened by the storm.

ANDREA GARNEY

Prayer is the key that shuts us up under
his protection and safeguard.

JACQUES ELLUL

This is a wise, sane Christian faith: that a man
commit himself, his life, and his hopes to God;
that God undertakes the special protection of
that man; that therefore that man ought not
to be afraid of anything.

GEORGE MACDONALD

Safe am I. Safe am I, in the hollow of His hand.

OLD SUNDAY SCHOOL SONG

He who keeps you will not slumber.
The LORD shall preserve you from all evil.

PSALM 121:3, 7

GOD'S LOVE

Jesus said, "It is your Father's good pleasure
to give you the kingdom."

LUKE 12:32

God loved you enough to send Jesus to die on the cross for you, in order to take away the sin that separated you from Him. Now you can look forward to eternal life in heaven.

But God doesn't stop there. As Paul asked, "He who did not spare His own Son ... how shall He not with Him also freely give us all things?" (Romans 8:32). God loves you enough to not only give you an unbelievably wonderful future in heaven, but also to do loving things for you here and now.

God is not a stingy Father. He is lavish and generous with His love. If you've been missing out on the benefits of being His child, draw near to Him today.

God's love is always supernatural, always a miracle, always the last thing we deserve.

ROBERT HORN

Jesus did not come to make God's love possible,
but to make God's love visible.

AUTHOR UNKNOWN

Every existing thing is equally upheld in
its existence by God's creative love.

SIMONE WEIL

God soon turns from his wrath,
but he never turns from his love.

CHARLES HADDON SPURGEON

Yes, I have loved you with an everlasting love.

JEREMIAH 31:3

SUCCESS

Remember the Lord in everything you do.
And he will give you success.

PROVERBS 3:6 NCV

It is God's will for you to succeed both in your spiritual life and in your daily labors. If you excel in your work but neglect your soul, you may end up with every material blessing, but find none of it satisfies. If you are deeply spiritual but unsuccessful and struggling in your work, you will be unable to properly provide for your family. God knows that both are important.

Success in one area of your life does not guarantee success in others, so always do your best and pray over every sphere of your life. God wants to bless you in every way. He wants you to succeed.

Three qualities vital to success:
toil, solitude, prayer.

CARL SANDBURG

Let us work as if success depended on ourselves alone, but with the heartfelt conviction that we are doing nothing and God everything.

SAINT IGNATIUS OF LOYOLA

I have only to be true to the highest I know— success or failure is in the hands of God.

E. STANLEY JONES

Success is a journey, not a destination.

BEN SWEETLAND

It is not that we think we can do anything of lasting value by ourselves.
Our only power and success come from God.

2 CORINTHIANS 3:5 NLT

MEDITATION

I meditate on You in the night watches.

PSALM 63:6

When you need to take a break from the busy rush of life and recharge your batteries, nothing works like meditation—focusing your thoughts on God. Get quiet for a few moments and reflect on God's greatness, His love, and His tenderness. Imagine Him creating the earth and all that dwells in it. Think for a while about the greatness of God in your own life. What has He done for you?

It's also productive to reflect on God's character—perfectly good, perfectly just, perfectly wise. As you meditate on God and His attributes, you will begin to feel you know Him better. You will gain new confidence to place yourself and your affairs in His care.

If we bring our minds back again and again to God, we shall be gradually giving the central place to God, not only in our inner selves, but in our practical everyday lives.

PAUL TOURNIER

Meditation is the activity of calling to mind,
and thinking over, and dwelling on, and applying
to oneself, the various things that one knows
about the works and ways and purposes
and promises of God.

J. I. PACKER

Enter the inner chamber of thy mind; shut out
all thoughts save that of God and such as can aid
thee in seeking him. Speak now, my whole heart!
Speak now to God, saying, "I seek thy face;
thy face, Lord, will I seek."

SAINT ANSELM

In the rush and noise of life, as you have
intervals, step home within yourselves and be still.
Wait upon God, and feel his good presence; this
will carry you evenly through your day's business.

WILLIAM PENN

I will meditate about your glory, splendor,
majesty, and miracles.

PSALM 145:5 TLB

FELLOWSHIP

If we are living in the light of God's presence,
just as Christ does, then we have wonderful fellowship
and joy with each other.

1 JOHN 1:7 TLB

It's acceptable to refer to any gathering as "fellowship," but the Bible uses the term to denote a depth of sharing and communion that is far rarer than it should be.

True fellowship is essential, because there are things God can do in you through the ministry of a body of believers that He seems to choose to do in no other way. Fellowship also provides the opportunity for you to exercise your spiritual gifts, something that cannot often be done outside an assembly of Christians.

Seek out the deep sharing and community that makes for true fellowship. It will draw you closer to your brothers and sisters—and to God.

We will win the world when we realize
that fellowship, not evangelism,
must be our primary emphasis.

JESS MOODY

No man is an island, entire of itself;
every man is a piece of the continent,
a part of the main.

JOHN DONNE

Be united with other Christians.
A wall with loose bricks is not good.
The bricks must be cemented together.

CORRIE TEN BOOM

What happens when God grants the gift of
genuine Christian fellowship? ... Sisters and
brothers begin to discuss the things that really
matter to them. They disclose their inner fears,
their areas of peculiar temptation,
their deepest joys.

RONALD J. SIDER

Do not be interested only in your own life,
but be interested in the lives of others.

PHILIPPIANS 2:4 NCV

SECURITY

They shall dwell safely,
and no one shall make them afraid.

EZEKIEL 34:28

Security is more than just locking up. Security also refers to anything you count on to provide for your family, such as putting savings in the bank or having a steady job, so you can pay your bills. There are practical steps you can take to make your life secure, and God requires you to take those steps.

Your ultimate security, however, is to have God looking out for you. That's why once you have done all you can, it is wise to pray and commit your security and well-being, and that of your family, into His hands.

God has not promised to protect you from every dip in the stock market or every downsizing in your workplace, but you are His child and He *has* promised He will always provide for you. You can rest securely in His care.

The saints in heaven are happier but no more secure than are true believers here in this world.

LORAINE BOETHNER

If your security is based on something that can be
taken away from you—you will constantly
be on a false edge of security.

TIM HANSEL

Security is not the absence of danger,
but the presence of God,
no matter what the danger.

AUTHOR UNKNOWN

No matter what may be the test,
God will take care of you.

C. D. MARTIN

*You can be sure that God will take care
of everything you need.*

PHILIPPIANS 4:19 THE MESSAGE

NATURE

*Jesus said, "Walk out into the fields
and look at the wildflowers."*

MATTHEW 6:28 THE MESSAGE

The Bible says the heavens and the earth proclaim the glory of God. They serve as evidence of His power and majesty. They confirm He is indeed great enough to handle your life— guiding you to the fulfillment of His plan and foiling any foe that might try to obstruct your path.

So look around you and see the glory of your God. Pause and consider the magnificence of a simple flower or the complexity of a common tree. Glance up at the sky and reflect on the fact God has created an atmosphere capable of sustaining your lives. Look at His handiwork and you will say as He did, "It is good."

We can almost smell the aroma of God's beauty
in the fresh spring flowers. His breath surrounds us
in the warm summer breezes.

GALE HEIDE

The more I study nature, the more I am amazed
at the Creator.

LOUIS PASTEUR

Nature is but a name for an effect
whose cause is God.

WILLIAM COWPER

I love to think of nature as an unlimited
broadcasting station through which God speaks
to us every hour, if we will only tune in.

GEORGE WASHINGTON CARVER

God's glory is on tour in the skies,
God-craft on exhibit across the horizon.

PSALM 19:1 THE MESSAGE

STRENGTH

The glory of young men is their strength.

PROVERBS 20:29

Talk about strength, God has *real* strength! You may work out at the gym every day and be in top physical form. You may be fit, healthy, and physically strong—but God can move mountains. There are no limits to God's strength.

So as you do your weight training, properly building up and improving your own physical strength, take advantage of the opportunity to remind yourself that God is stronger than you will ever be. He is strong enough to meet any need you might have—physical, emotion, or spiritual. No matter how strong you may be, you will always be strong enough when God adds His muscle to yours.

When a man has no strength, if he leans on God, he becomes powerful.

DWIGHT L. MOODY

When God is our strength, it is strength indeed;
when our strength is our own, it is only weakness.

SAINT AUGUSTINE OF HIPPO

The Lord doesn't promise to give us something to
take so we can handle our weary moments.
He promises us himself. That is all.
And that is enough.

CHARLES R. SWINDOLL

The weaker we feel, the harder we lean on God.
And the harder we lean, the stronger we grow.

JONI EARECKSON TADA

Blessed is the man whose strength is in You ...
They go from strength to strength.

PSALM 84:5, 7

PRIORITIES

Jesus said, "These you ought to have done,
without leaving the others undone."

MATTHEW 23:23 THE MESSAGE

Do you have a clear understanding of what is most important in life? Jesus said that it was more important to store treasure in heaven than to seek earthly riches. He instructed His disciples to put the things of God before even their physical needs.

The good news is that once you know what to put at the top of your list, it's easier to decide what to do with the rest. Would God want me to put my work ahead of my family's needs? Is God pleased when I make money my first concern?

God wants you to have a good life, filled with love, peace, and joy. When you let Him help you get your priorities in order, you can bet that's where you're headed.

When first things are put first,
second things are not suppressed but increased.

C. S. LEWIS

When you put God first, you are establishing
order for everything else in your life.

ANDREA GARNEY

Tell me to what you pay attention,
and I will tell you who you are.

JOSÉ ORTEGA Y GASSET

Do not let the good things in life rob you
of the best things.

BUSTER ROTHMAN

Let all things be done decently and in order.

1 CORINTHIANS 14:40

PEACE

*The peace of God, which surpasses all understanding,
will guard your hearts and minds through Christ Jesus.*
PHILIPPIANS 4:7

It's not hard to be relaxed and peaceful when everything is going smoothly and your problems are all under control. But that's not real peace. Real peace is the inner calm God's Spirit gives when the world around you is chaotic, stress is bearing down on you, and things are going right off the rails at work and at home.

You get that kind of peace by trusting God and keeping your heart focused on Him. In return, His peace will keep you calm and under control—making you better able to process solutions and deal effectively with circumstances. Don't settle for a fragile peace that can't handle all life is handing you. Put your hand in God's hand.

Christ alone can bring lasting peace—
peace with God—peace among men
and nations—and peace within our hearts.

BILLY GRAHAM

No God, no peace. Know God, know peace.

AUTHOR UNKNOWN

At the heart of the cyclone tearing the sky
And flinging the clouds and the towers by,
Is a place of central calm;…
In the hollow of God's palm.

EDWIN MARKHAM

If the basis of peace is God,
the secret of peace is trust.

J. N. FIGGIS

You will keep him in perfect peace,
whose mind is stayed on You.

ISAIAH 26:3 THE MESSAGE

JOY

Celebrate God all day, every day.
I mean, revel in him!

PHILIPPIANS 4:4 THE MESSAGE

God knows some people are cheerful and expressive by nature and others more serious and quiet. Yet He tells *all* Christians—including you—to rejoice! What's the deal?

Joy is not necessarily wild exuberance, but rather, a steady, enduring inner happiness. It is anchored in God, who is seated high above the circumstances of your life. As long as you are holding on to Him, you can be joyful even in the midst of sadness and distress. King David was.

Even when David's enemies were hunting him down and closing in, he was able to compose joyful psalms of praise to God. He rejoiced in his understanding that God, His Father, could flatten any army, resolve any conflict, and confuse the plans of those who sought to kill him. He was joyful in the Lord.

Joy is an unceasing fountain bubbling up in the heart; a secret spring the world can't see and doesn't know anything about.

DWIGHT L. MOODY

Joy is the most infallible sign of
the presence of God.

LEON BLOY

Life need not be easy to be joyful.
Joy is not the absence of trouble
but the presence of Christ.

WILLIAM VAN DER HOVEN

Happiness depends on what happens;
joy does not.

OSWALD CHAMBERS

Rejoice always.

1 THESSALONIANS 5:16

WISDOM

*The LORD gives wisdom; from His mouth
come knowledge and understanding.*

PROVERBS 2:6

It's good to have knowledge, but just knowing facts and figures won't make you a better man. Knowing what to *do* with the information you have—wisdom—has the power to change your life and the lives of others.

People gain conventional wisdom as they go through life, primarily by learning from their mistakes. Godly wisdom, however, is a gift from God. Solomon, the biblical king known for his wisdom, received his insights in this way. He simply asked.

You can ask for wisdom too. God knows you will face confusing situations at times. If you ask, He has promised to give you the wisdom you need.

Wisdom is the application of knowledge.

AUTHOR UNKNOWN

The next best thing to being wise oneself is
to live in a circle of those who are.

C. S. LEWIS

Wisdom is concerned with how we relate
to people, to the world, and to God.

EDMUND P. CLOWNEY

Wisdom is a gift direct from God.

BOB JONES

Above all and before all, do this:
Get Wisdom!

PROVERBS 4:6 THE MESSAGE

REST

Jesus said, "Come off by yourselves;
let's take a break and get a little rest."

MARK 6:31 THE MESSAGE

Jesus knew what it was like to be busy. The Bible says He ministered to the poor, the sick, and the spiritually needy from dawn to dusk. That's why He insisted on taking a breather. He knew neither He nor His disciples could keep up the pace without taking time out for a rest. And He knows you need rest too.

So, when you feel yourself getting impatient and frayed around the edges, stop for a while. Let your mind and body catch up. God will bless your work even more when you get back to it. Many find their creativity, problem-solving abilities, and coping skills all get a kick upward when they return after even a five- or ten-minute break.

Jesus knows we must come apart and rest a while,
or else we may just plain come apart.

VANCE HAVNER

Life lived amidst tension and busyness needs
leisure—leisure that re-creates and renews.

NEIL C. STRAIT

Take rest; a field that has rested gives
a bountiful crop.

OVID

How beautiful it is to do nothing,
and then rest afterward.

SPANISH PROVERB

Jesus said, "Come to Me, all you who labor
and are heavy laden, and I will give you rest."

MATTHEW 11:28

HEAVEN

From that time Jesus began to preach and to say,
"Repent, for the kingdom of heaven is at hand."

MATTHEW 4:17

Simply stated, heaven is this: to know the only true God—God the Father and His Son, Jesus Christ, whom He has sent. After death, Christians will know the delight of God's full presence. That will be heaven.

But did you know you can feel the delight of God's presence here on Earth? When you spend time with God in prayer, read the words He's written to you in the Bible, and spend time meditating on His greatness, you are experiencing a foretaste of what it will be like in your heavenly home. Remember it, relish it, close your eyes and let yourself be enveloped by God's loving presence. It is your future, your eternity.

Heaven is a prepared place for a prepared people.

LEWIS SPERRY CHAFER

Earth has no sorrow that heaven cannot heal.

THOMAS V. MOORE

Heaven will be the perfection we have always longed for. All the things that made earth unlovely and tragic will be absent in heaven.

BILLY GRAHAM

God's retirement plan is out of this world.

AUTHOR UNKNOWN

He puts a little of heaven in our hearts
so that we'll never settle for less.

2 CORINTHIANS 5:5 THE MESSAGE

HELP

Our soul waits for the LORD;
He is our help and our shield.

Say you're in your backyard learning how to cast your new fishing rod. You encounter a problem, so you call an expert-fisherman friend to come over and help. He arrives, takes the rod out of your hand, and says, "I'll take it from here. Go on inside." Walking up your back steps you hear him shout, "And from now on, don't try casting this yourself. I'll do all your casting for you." As the screen door slams behind you, you think, *All I wanted was a little help.*

God is always there to help you, not to elbow you out of your own life. When you think about it, you wouldn't want it any other way.

What other help could we ever need than that of the Holy Spirit of God?

ANDREA GARNEY

Call the Comforter by the term you think best—
Advocate, Helper, Paraclete, the word conveys
the indefinable blessedness of his sympathy;
an inward invisible kingdom that causes the saint
to sing through every night of sorrow.

OSWALD CHAMBERS

The Holy Spirit has promised to lead us
step by step into the fullness of truth.

LEON JOSEPH SUENENS

Jesus promised his followers that
"The Strengthener" would be with them.
This promise is no lullaby for the fainthearted.
It is a blood transfusion for courageous living.

E. PAUL HOVEY

We can feel sure and say,
"I will not be afraid because the Lord is my helper."

HEBREWS 13:6 NCV

TRUTH

*Jesus said, "You shall know the truth,
and the truth shall make you free."*

JOHN 8:32

The Bible says fear can make you a captive—
and truth can set you free. What truth is it
that has this amazing power over fear? The truth that
Jesus Christ has conquered sin, death, and the grave.
He has mastered every situation you could possibly
face, forgiven every sin you could possibly commit,
and given you eternal life.

So why would you choose to stay inside your
prison cell? Take hold of the truth. Meditate on it
until you see the doors swinging open before you. You
are free to go, to live, to thrive, to love, to be loved,
to be fulfilled as a man. And that's the truth!

No truths are simple, especially those of Scripture.
But as we pursue them and participate in them
more fully, they begin to reveal to us a life
deeper and more integrated than we ever
could have known otherwise.

TIM HANSEL

Man finds God through truth.

JEWISH PROVERB

A person can be free even within prison walls.
Freedom is something spiritual.
Whoever has once had it, can never lose it.

BERTOLT BRECHT

The man who finds a truth lights a torch.

ROBERT GREEN INGERSOLL

Lead me in Your truth and teach me,
for You are the God of my salvation.
On You I wait all the day.

PSALM 25:5

HUMILITY

Jesus said, "Whoever exalts himself will be humbled, and he who humbles himself will be exalted."

LUKE 14:11

Many people associate humility with false modesty, denigrating yourself and talking down your accomplishments before others. That couldn't be further from the truth. Humility is really just the freedom to be the man God created you to be—nothing more, nothing less. It's a license to stop pretending.

God knows exactly who you are, and He likes you. He would never ask you to represent yourself as less than His marvelous creation. What He does ask you to do is to be exactly who you are—no prideful extensions, no hokey denials. That's humility—the real you, up close and personal.

For those who would learn God's ways, humility is the first thing, humility is the second, humility is the third.

SAINT AUGUSTINE OF HIPPO

If you are humble, nothing will touch you,
neither praise nor disgrace,
because you know what you are.

MOTHER TERESA

It is no great thing to be humble when you
are brought low; but to be humble when
you are praised is a great and rare attainment.

SAINT BERNARD OF CLAIRVAUX

Humility is nothing else but a true knowledge
and awareness of oneself as one really is.

THE CLOUD OF UNKNOWING

Be clothed with humility, for "God resists the proud,
but gives grace to the humble."

1 PETER 5:5

INTEGRITY

*Jesus said, "There's trouble ahead when you live
only for the approval of others. ...
Your task is to be true, not popular."*

LUKE 6:26 THE MESSAGE

Many men suffer from chronic performance
anxiety. Is that the case with you? Are
you constantly wondering what kind of reviews you
will receive from your wife, your children, you boss,
your friends, your co-workers? If so, here's a little
stage wisdom to help you cope.

Kill the foot lights and turn up the house lights.
When you do, you will see there is only one VIP in
the audience—God. Ultimately, His review is the
only one that matters. When you live your life in a
manner pleasing to Him, the other people in your life
will be pleased as well. So chase away your anxiety
and live a life of unwavering integrity. You're bound
to be a hit!

God is the only goal worthy of man's efforts.

SAINT AUGUSTINE OF HIPPO

God expects of us only what he has himself
first supplied. He is quick to mark every
simple effort to please him, and just as quick
to overlook imperfections when he knows
we meant to do his will.

A. W. TOZER

There is no work better than another to please
God; to pour water, to wash dishes, to be a cobbler,
or an apostle, all is one; to wash dishes
and to preach is all one, as touching as the deed,
to please God.

WILLIAM TYNDALE

What kind of habitation pleases God?
What must our natures be like before he can feel
at home within us? He asks nothing but
a pure heart and a single mind. ... He desires
but sincerity, transparency, humility, and love.
He will see to the rest.

A. W. TOZER

Whoever finds me [Wisdom] finds life
and wins approval from the Lord.

PROVERBS 8:35 TLB

GOALS

*Forgetting those things which are behind and reaching
forward to those things which are ahead,
I press toward the goal for the prize of
the upward call of God in Christ Jesus.*

PHILIPPIANS 3:13–14

Ask any successful runner where he focuses his attention during a race. He'll tell you he does not watch his competitors, his feet, or the crowd. Rather, his attention stays fixed on the finish line. He focuses on his goal—and that disciplined focus leads him to victory.

If you desire to make the most of the life God has given you, you must be able to focus on your goal as well. Ask God to reveal His plan for your life. Ask Him to help you see the markers along the way. Then, lace up your running shoes and go for it. God will be with you throughout the race. And He will be there to present you with your prize when you cross the finish line.

The goal of a virtuous life is to become like God.

GREGORY OF NYSSA

The tragedy in life doesn't lie in not reaching your goal. The tragedy lies in having no goal to reach.

BENJAMIN MAYS

You become successful the moment you start moving toward a worthwhile goal.

AUTHOR UNKNOWN

First build a proper goal. That proper goal will make it easy, almost automatic, to build a proper you.

JOHANN WOLFGANG VON GOETHE

*Let us fix our eyes on Jesus,
the author and perfecter of our faith.*

HEBREWS 12:2 NIV

GUIDANCE

Jesus said, "When He, the Spirit of truth, has come, He will guide you into all truth."

JOHN 16:13

Imagine yourself standing on the edge of a field of land mines, wondering how you'll get across to safety. Suddenly, someone appears who tells you he knows where all the mines are. "I can lead you through safely," he says. How would you answer? Would you say, "No thanks. I don't need your help." Of course not. More likely you would say, "Thanks. I'll follow and stay close."

God knows life can be like a big field of land mines. He knows—and He wants to help you get to the other side safely. He will never impose His ways on you, but you would be wise to follow and stay close.

All the way my Savior leads me; what have I to ask beside? Can I doubt His tender mercy, who through life has been my guide.

FRANCES JANE VAN ALSTYNE

Deep in your heart it is not guidance that
you want as much as a guide.

JOHN WHITE

I know not the way God leads me,
but well do I know my Guide.

MARTIN LUTHER

The teacher of teachers gives his guidance
noiselessly. I have never heard him speak,
and yet I know that he is within me.
At every moment he instructs me and guides me.
And whenever I am in need of it,
he enlightens me afresh.

THERESE OF LISIEUX

Your ears shall hear a word behind you, saying,
"This is the way, walk in it," whenever you turn
to the right hand or whenever you turn to the left.

ISAIAH 30:21

HOPE

*May the God of hope fill you with all joy and peace
in believing, that you may abound
in hope by the power of the Holy Spirit.*

ROMANS 15:13

Imagine for a moment how hopeless the followers of Jesus Christ must have felt as they wrapped His lifeless body in grave clothes and laid it in a borrowed tomb. Jesus had tried to tell them what was coming. He tried to make them understand they would see Him again, that He would return to them, but they simply could not take hold.

Hope replaced despair, however, when they saw Jesus standing before them—risen from the dead. Christ's resurrection from the dead holds the key to your hope as well. Because He is alive, you have hope of life after death, hope of one day again seeing your loved ones who have died in the Lord, hope of spending eternity in a place where our loving God rules and reigns.

Hope can see heaven through the thickest clouds.

THOMAS BENTON BROOKS

Do not look to your hope, but to Christ,
the source of your hope.

CHARLES HADDON SPURGEON

Hope means faith in God
and in His omnipotence.

CARLO CARRETTO

Hope is the struggle of the soul,
breaking loose from what is perishable
and attesting her eternity.

HERMAN MELVILLE

Put all your hope in how kind God will be to you
when Jesus Christ appears.

1 PETER 1:13 CEV

WHOLENESS

Jesus answered and said to them, "Those who are well
have no need of a physician, but those who are sick.
I have not come to call the righteous,
but sinners, to repentance."

LUKE 5:31–32

When Jesus and His disciples walked
through the hill country of Nazareth, He
ministered to all who came to Him. He touched
those who needed healing and made them well. He
healed those whose minds were sick and failing. But
Jesus also spoke of those who needed spiritual
healing—those whose souls were sick with sin and
on the verge of spiritual death. Jesus brought healing
to every part of His followers' lives.

Perhaps your body is fit and healthy, your mind
quick and strong, but you have no relationship with
God. Your spirit has been mortally wounded and only
God can make you whole again. Seek Him out. Tell
Him what you need. He's the Great Physician.

The part can never be well unless
the whole is well.

PLATO

To be "whole" is to be spiritually, emotionally,
and physically healthy.
Jesus lived in perfect wholeness.

COLIN URQUHART

He who has health has hope,
and he who has hope has everything.

ARAB PROVERB

Our prayers should be for a sound mind
in a healthy body.

JUVENAL

*I wish above all things that thou mayest prosper
and be in health, even as thy soul prospereth.*

3 JOHN 2 KJV

DECISIONS

*Trust in the LORD with all your heart, and
lean not on your own understanding; in all your ways
acknowledge Him, and He shall direct your paths.*

PROVERBS 3:5–6

People say they want to make their own decisions, set their own course. But being a decision maker can be tough. After all, the world is constantly changing. You may have a bead on the past and the present, but the future is anyone's guess.

Unless ... you happen to know the One who knows the future. No—He isn't the great fortune teller in the sky, but He will give you the wisdom you need to make good choices. He will show you timeless principles in the Bible and lead you to wise people who can help you put things into proper perspective. And when you've made the right decision, He'll fill your heart with His peace.

In making our decisions, we must use the brains
that God has given us. But we must also use
our hearts which He also gave us.

FULTON OURSLER

If we are ever in doubt about what to do,
it is a good rule to ask ourselves what we shall wish
on the morrow that we had done.

SIR JOHN LUBBOCK

There is a time when we must firmly choose
the course we will follow, or the relentless drift of
events will make the decision.

HERBERT V. PROCHNOW

When you are rightly related to God ...
you decide things in perfect delightful friendship
with God, knowing that if your decisions
are wrong he will always check.
When he checks, stop at once.

OSWALD CHAMBERS

*If you need wisdom—if you want to know
what God wants you to do—ask him,
and he will gladly tell you.*

JAMES 1:5 NLT

ACCEPTANCE

He made us accepted in the Beloved.

Many people search their entire lives for the acceptance of others. They strive to wear the right clothes, do the right things, speak the right words—all in an attempt to make others like them. Are you one of those people?

If so, you are searching for something you already have. God created you, and He accepts you just the way you are. There is nothing you can do or say or think that will make Him love you more than He already does.

It's all right to want others to like you—but you aren't likely to find what you really desire until you see yourself as God sees you.

Acceptance means you are valuable
just as you are. It allows you to be the real you.

Be absolutely certain that our Lord loves you,
devotedly and individually, loves you
just as you are. ... Accustom yourself to
the wonderful thought that God loves you
with a tenderness, a generosity, and an intimacy
that surpasses all your dreams.

ABBE HENRI DE TOURVILLE

God carries your picture in his wallet.

TONY CAMPOLO

Just as I am, thou wilt receive, will welcome,
pardon, cleanse, relieve; because thy promise
I believe, O Lamb of God, I come.

CHARLOTTE ELLIOTT

Honor God by accepting each other,
as Christ has accepted you.

ROMANS 15:7 CEV

GENTLENESS

You have also given me the shield of Your salvation;
Your right hand has held me up,
Your gentleness has made me great.

PSALM 18:35

The Bible speaks of Jesus Christ as the Lion of the tribe of Judah. It's quite a daunting title—fierce, commanding. And yet, Jesus told His disciples that He was "gentle and humble in heart" (Matt. 11:29 NIV). Which description is true? Both.

You may think gentleness equates to weakness. But that simply isn't so. Gentleness is actually controlled strength. It is the ability to choose to reach out to another person with tenderness and caring when it is within your power to crush and destroy.

Choose to be gentle with those whom God has placed in your life—your spouse, your children, your coworkers. In that way, you will be following in the footsteps of Jesus.

When you encounter difficulties
and contradictions, do not try to break them,
but bend them with gentleness and time.

SAINT FRANCIS DE SALES

True gentleness is founded on a sense of
what we owe to Him who made us
and to the common nature, which we all share.

HUGH BLAIR

There is nothing stronger in the world
than gentleness.

HAN SUYIN

Only the weak are cruel.
Gentleness can only be expected from the strong.

LEO BUSCAGLIA

Let your gentleness be known to all men.
The Lord is at hand.

PHILIPPIANS 4:5

ASSURANCE

Whoever calls on the name of the LORD shall be saved.
ACTS 2:21

Some people believe you can't be certain of your salvation until after you die. But the New Testament is filled with assurances—God's deep desire is for everyone to receive the gift of salvation, Christ's sacrifice on the cross was sufficient to cover all sin, any person who is forgiven and cleansed by Christ's blood is heir to eternal life.

God doesn't want you to live your life *wondering* if you will make it to heaven. He wants you to *know* He is preparing a place for you. Jesus said to the thief who hung beside Him on the cross, "This day you will be with me in paradise." That day, with his dying breath, a criminal turned to Jesus and received the assurance of his salvation.

The assurance of salvation is one of God's beautiful gifts. Every believer ought to know that he possesses salvation.

GEORGE SWEETING

You may be assured that you have life eternal for
"he that hath the Son hath life."

H. A. IRONSIDE

You should not believe your conscience
and your feelings more than the word that
the Lord who receives sinners preaches to you.

MARTIN LUTHER

Since no man is excluded from calling upon God
the gate of salvation is set open to all.
There is nothing else to hinder us from entering,
but our own unbelief.

JOHN CALVIN

These things I have written to you who believe in
the name of the Son of God, that you may know that
you have eternal life, and that you may continue
to believe in the name of the Son of God.

1 JOHN 5:13

BLESSINGS

*Blessed be the God and Father of our Lord
Jesus Christ, who has blessed us with every
spiritual blessing in the heavenly places in Christ.*

EPHESIANS 1:3

Blessing is the currency of the kingdom of God. When He created man and woman and set them on the earth, He blessed them with an abundance of cool clear water, fresh air, and fertile soil. When men and women turn to God and open their hearts to Him, another layer of blessing is applied—eternal life, forgiveness of sin, the love of a caring heavenly Father. And that's not all!

There are also blessings that come as a result of obeying the principles in God's Word. The Bible says to obey God's commandments and you will be blessed. Share generously with the poor and you will be blessed. Honor your father and mother and you will be blessed.

Reach out to God. He wants to bless you!

Let never day nor night unhallow'd pass,
but still remember what the Lord hath done.

WILLIAM SHAKESPEARE

Count your many blessings, angels will attend,
help and comfort give you to your journey's end.
JOHNSON OATMAN JR.

God particularly pours out his blessings upon
those who know how much they need him.
ROBERT HAROLD SCHULLER

God is more anxious to bestow his blessings
on us than we are to receive them.
SAINT AUGUSTINE OF HIPPO

I will send down showers in season;
there will be showers of blessing.
EZEKIEL 34:26 NIV

GOODNESS

He saved us, not because of the good things we did,
but because of his mercy. He washed away our sins
and gave us a new life through the Holy Spirit.

TITUS 3:5 NLT

Do you believe being good will get you into heaven? That sounds right, but, in fact, it is wrong. Being a "good" man won't do it. To measure up to God's standard, you must be more than good; you must be *perfect*—and human beings just aren't capable of that.

That's why God sent His Son, Jesus Christ, to live a life of perfect goodness—a life completely pleasing to God—and then sacrifice that perfect life for you. Don't count on being good enough to spend eternity with God. You'll never make it. Instead, count on the goodness of Christ—God's perfect Son—to get you there.

God cannot accept goodness from me.
He can only accept my badness,
and he will give me the solid goodness of
the Lord Jesus in exchange for it.

OSWALD CHAMBERS

We please Him [God] most, not by frantically
trying to make ourselves good, but by throwing
ourselves into His arms with all our imperfections,
and believing that He understands
everything and loves us still.

A. W. TOZER

We must first be made good before
we can do good; we must first be made just,
before our works can please God.

HUGH LATIMER

To do good is human; to be good is divine.

JAMES MARTINEAU

When wisdom enters your heart, and knowledge
is pleasant to your soul, ...
you may walk in the way of goodness.

PROVERBS 2:10, 20

BELIEF

Belief is not the absence of doubt, but the decision to stand in the midst of your doubts. Thomas had his doubts when the other disciples told him Jesus had risen from the dead. But when Jesus appeared, He never condemned Thomas. Instead, He gave him evidence. He encouraged Thomas to touch Him and believe.

God doesn't condemn you for your doubts either. He just wants you to reach out to Him, to let Him prove to you He does indeed exist. He desires to win you with His love and draw you with His kindness. Bring your doubts to Jesus; lay them at His feet in prayer. Let Him turn your doubts to belief.

No man ever believes with a true and saving faith
unless God inclines his heart;
and no man when God does incline his heart
can refrain from believing.

BLAISE PASCAL

Faith never means gullibility. The man who
believes everything is as far from God
as the man who refuses to believe anything.

A. W. TOZER

God alone can make a man a believer.
Our part is to accept or reject his initiative.

JOHN POWELL

To believe in God is to believe in someone who
will always be far beyond us, who will forever be
presenting a new aspect of himself to us.

LOUIS EVELY

He that cometh to God must believe that he is,
and that he is a rewarder of them
that diligently seek him.

HEBREWS 11:6 KJV

CHILDREN

Children are a heritage from the LORD, the fruit of
the womb a reward. As arrows are in the hand of
a warrior, so are the children of one's youth.

PSALM 127:3–4

"Once a parent, always a parent," as the wise old saying goes. If you have children of any age, you know they will always be in your heart. God never intended parenting to be an "until you're grown and out of the house" proposition. He meant it to last a lifetime. Yes, indeed, the relationship changes, but it never disappears.

God wants you to know you will always be His child. As you grow and mature, there will be times of discipline, times of instruction, times of close parental care. And as you grow older, there will be times of blessed friendship and sweet communion with your Father God. Your relationship will change with time, but it will last for eternity.

Ideal parenting is modeled after the relationship
between God and man.

JAMES DOBSON

The overwhelming majority in our churches today were converted before twenty-one years of age. Whatever your church does, let it do its duty by the children.

R. A. TORREY

Call not that man wretched, who, whatever else he suffers as to pain inflicted or pleasure denied, has a child for whom he hopes and on whom he dotes.

SAMUEL TAYLOR COLERIDGE

Children are God's apostles, day by day sent forth to preach of love and hope and peace.

JAMES RUSSELL LOWELL

Jesus said, "Let the little children come to Me,
and do not forbid them;
for of such is the kingdom of heaven."

MATTHEW 19:14

EXPECTANCY

The eyes of all look expectantly to You,
and You give them their food in due season.

PSALM 145:15

One of the most exciting things about having a relationship with God is that there is always more on the horizon. The life of a believer is a life of expectancy. A. B. Simpson was once asked if he believed in a "second blessing" experience after salvation. "Yes," he replied, "and a third and fourth! God always has more for you."

Just as He provided the children of Israel with fresh manna to eat each morning, God's mercies are new for you each morning as well. Don't dwell in the past. Wait expectantly for the manna God has for you today. You won't be disappointed.

Complacency is a deadly foe of all spiritual growth.
Acute desire must be present or there will be
no manifestation of Christ to His people.
He waits to be wanted.

A. W. TOZER

When one door closes, another opens;
but we often look so long and so regretfully
upon the closed door that we do not see
the one which has opened for us.

ALEXANDER GRAHAM BELL

'Tis expectation makes a blessing dear.

SIR JOHN SUCKLING

There is something new every day
if you look for it.

HANNAH HURNARD

In the morning, O LORD, you hear my voice;
in the morning I lay my requests before you
and wait in expectation.

PSALM 5:3 NIV

ETERNAL LIFE

Jesus said, "I am the resurrection and the life.
He who believes in Me, though he may die,
he shall live. And whoever lives
and believes in Me shall never die."

JOHN 11:25–26

When you hear the phrase "eternal life," you probably think of heaven, which is understandable. But you do not have to wait for heaven; eternal life begins now, the moment you receive Christ as Savior. This means your life has a new dimension—an eternal, undying quality it never had before. From now on, everything is a prelude, a dress rehearsal for your heavenly future.

This perspective will change your priorities and purpose. Some activities will become less important in light of heavenly values. Deadlines, worries, and time restraints will not be oppressive to the man who has a heavenly view. Spend your day with the conscious knowledge of eternal life, and see the difference it makes!

God has set the quality of everlastingness
in our hearts.

A. W. TOZER

Even here and now, whenever the heart begins
to burn with a desire for God, she is made able to
receive the uncreated light and, inspired
and fulfilled by the gifts of the Holy Ghost,
she tastes the joys of heaven. She transcends
all visible things and is raised to
the sweetness of eternal life.

RICHARD ROLLE OF HAMPOLE

Eternal life does not begin with death;
it begins with faith.

SAMUEL M. SHOEMAKER

Eternity to the godly is a day that has no sunset.

THOMAS WATSON

*Jesus said, "Whoever believes in the Son
has eternal life."*

JOHN 3:36 NRSV

CONTENTMENT

Godliness with contentment is great gain.
1 TIMOTHY 6:6

You may find contentment to be one of the more difficult Christian virtues to develop. Every day you are bombarded with advertising messages that, by and large, seek to make you discontent so you can be persuaded to fill your newfound need with some new possession.

Think of it this way: contentment is a by-product of thankfulness. Set aside some time each day to thank God for all He has done for you. Verbalize your thanks. Count your blessings, one by one, thanking God for each and every gift. Soon you will have a new appreciation for what you have, rather than discouragement over what you don't have.

A contented mind is a continual feast.
PROVERB

We should be content with what we have,
but never with what we are.

CHANNING POLLOCK

A contented man is the one who enjoys
the scenery along the detours.

AUTHOR UNKNOWN

Being "contented" ought to mean in English,
as it does in French, being pleased.

G. K. CHESTERTON

I have learned to be content with whatever I have.
PHILIPPIANS 4:11 NRSV

CHURCH

*Let us consider one another in order to stir up love
and good works, not forsaking the assembling of
ourselves together, as is the manner of some,
but exhorting one another, and so much
the more as you see the Day approaching.*

HEBREWS 10:24–25

You can't be a part of a church fellowship for very long without encountering conflict. The church is made up of people—imperfect human beings just like you. God doesn't expect you to pretend it isn't so. Instead, He asks you to love and forgive and join hands.

If you are feeling frustrated by the conflict in your church, pray for the grace to show love to your brothers and sisters in Christ. Ask God to bring unity, beginning with your own heart. One day in heaven, God's Church—those whom He has redeemed—will be united in every way, as flawless as a bride on her wedding day. But for now, God asks you to be kind, humble, loving, and forgiving.

A church is a hospital for sinners,
not a museum for saints.

L. L. NASH

Church-goers are like coals in a fire.
When they cling together, they keep
the flame aglow; when they separate,
they die out.

BILLY GRAHAM

Church attendance is as vital to a disciple
as a transfusion of rich, healthy blood
to a sick man.

DWIGHT L. MOODY

If you want to join a church with no problems ...
don't—you'll ruin it.

CHARLES R. SWINDOLL

God's household ... is the church of the living God,
the pillar and foundation of the truth.

1 TIMOTHY 3:15 NIV

GOD'S FAITHFULNESS

If we are faithless, He remains faithful;
He cannot deny Himself.

2 TIMOTHY 2:13

God's faithfulness grows out of the unchanging perfection of His nature. Because He is infinite and perfect in His love, mercy, and kindness, you can trust Him to be perfectly faithful in His care for you. Your friends may fail you; your own heart may fail you, but God never will. Divine faithfulness is just God being what He has always been and always will be.

That is why it is foolishness to think for a moment God's faithfulness to you is in any way dependent upon your performance. Even if you have been faithless, turn your heart to the One who is ever faithful. He is always ready to take you in.

Upon God's faithfulness rests our whole hope of future blessedness.

A. W. TOZER

What more powerful consideration can be
thought on to make us true to God,
than the faithfulness and truth of God to us?

WILLIAM GURNALL

Whoever falls from God's right hand
is caught into his left.

EDWIN MARKHAM

Though men are false, God is faithful.

MATTHEW HENRY

The Lord is faithful, who will establish you
and guard you from the evil one.

2 THESSALONIANS 3:3

BENEVOLENCE

What is desired in a man is kindness.

PROVERBS 19:22

You may think of benevolence only in terms of giving money, but there is much more to it than that. Benevolence is simply showing kindness; and in many cases, it is more a matter of opening your heart than your wallet.

In an age of hardness and cruelty, practicing benevolence is more difficult, but also more crucial. So many people are suffering for lack of a helping hand. Give to others with the same open-handed freedom God has given to you. Do it out of your love for Him and in a spirit of thankfulness for what you have received from Him. He will bless you for it many times over.

The heart benevolent and kind
the most resembles God.

ROBERT BURNS

There cannot be a more glorious object in creation than a human being replete with benevolence, meditating in what manner he may render himself most acceptable to the Creator by doing good to his creatures.

HENRY FIELDING

That best portion of a good man's life,
His little, nameless unremembered acts
Of kindness and love.

WILLIAM WORDSWORTH

The true source of cheerfulness is benevolence. The soul that perpetually overflows with kindness and sympathy will always be cheerful.

PARKE GODWIN

It is more blessed to give than to receive.

ACTS 20:35 KJV

GRACE

In him we have redemption through his blood,
the forgiveness of sins,
according to the riches of his grace.

Would you develop a relationship with someone who could bring nothing to the relationship? If it were all give and no take, would you even bother?

Now consider the fact that God's relationship with you is just that way. He created everything—there is nothing you can give Him He does not already have. That's what grace is all about. It is unmerited favor. God gives you what you do not deserve, knowing full well you can never pay Him back. All you have is from His hand, through His matchless, infinite grace.

Will you be God's hand of grace extended to others?

Grace means the free, unmerited, unexpected love of God, and all the benefits, delights, and comforts, which flow from it. It means that while we were sinners and enemies we have been treated as sons and heirs.

R .P. C. HANSON

God's grace says, "I've picked up the tab. I'll take care of everything inside and out. Accept it. Believe it. It's a declared fact."

CHARLES R. SWINDOLL

Grace is God's goodness, the kindness of God's heart, the good will, the cordial benevolence. It is what God is like. God is like that all the time.

A. W. TOZER

There is nothing but God's grace. We walk upon it; we breathe it; we live and die by it; it makes the nails and axles of the universe.

ROBERT LOUIS STEVENSON

You have been saved by grace because you believe. You did not save yourselves. It was a gift from God.

EPHESIANS 2:8 NCV

FRIENDSHIP

*A friend loves at all times,
and a brother is born for adversity.*

PROVERBS 17:17

You may have heard of the counseling theory that suggests you limit your friendships to "safe" people—those with no emotional baggage that could drag you down. That doesn't sound right, does it? Not only could this severely limit your pool of potential friends, but it seems to violate the selfless example of Christ, who specialized in making friends of those who were down and out.

You could be a great influence for good in a needy person's life, simply by making friends with them. Certainly some people can be emotionally draining, and you should always ask God for wisdom when approaching a new relationship. He will always steer you in the right direction. And He will often point you to diamonds in the rough.

A real friend is one who walks in when
the rest of the world walks out.

WALTER WINCHELL

Friendship is one of the sweetest joys of life.
Many might have failed beneath the bitterness of
their trial had they not found a friend.

CHARLES HADDON SPURGEON

It brings comfort to have companions
in whatever happens.

SAINT JOHN CHRYSOSTOM

You can make more friends in two months by
becoming interested in other people than
you can in two years by trying to get
other people interested in you.

DALE CARNEGIE

A man that hath friends must shew himself friendly.
PROVERBS 18:24 KJV

FUTURE

Since future victory is sure, be strong and steady,
always abounding in the Lord's work.

1 CORINTHIANS 15:58 TLB

There are two ways of looking at the future. You can worry yourself silly, or you can place your future in the hands of God and walk forward with confidence and courage. It isn't that God wants you to be unconcerned about the future. Jesus urged His disciples to plan and prepare for what was ahead of them. But He also told them not to be consumed with worry.

God has a wonderful plan for your life—whether you are fifteen or fifty-five. He wants you to fearlessly face each day with your hand in His. Don't allow what *might* happen to rob you of your sense of excitement and anticipation. Go forward into the future with God.

I've read the last page of the Bible.
It's all going to turn out all right.

BILLY GRAHAM

The future is as bright as the promises of God.

WILLIAM CAREY

Never be afraid to trust an unknown future
to a known God.

CORRIE TEN BOOM

Many live in dread of what is coming.
Why should we? The unknown puts adventure
into life. It gives us something to sharpen our
souls on. The unexpected around the corner
gives a sense of anticipation and surprise.
Thank God for the unknown future.

E. STANLEY JONES

For the good man—the blameless, the upright,
the man of peace—he has a wonderful future ahead of
him. For him there is a happy ending.

PSALM 37:37 TLB

COMFORT

Blessed be the God and Father of our Lord Jesus
Christ, the Father of mercies and God of all comfort,
who comforts us in all our tribulation, that we may be
able to comfort those who are in any trouble,
with the comfort with which we ourselves
are comforted by God.

2 CORINTHIANS 1:3–4

When you are going through tough times, you may wonder why God allows it. Only God knows the reasons. What you can be sure of is He will be there for you, no matter what circumstance you encounter. His love and comfort are resources that will see you through your trial.

And don't forget others are watching as you lean on God's comforting arm in the face of heartache and disappointment. Your example may show them where to turn when they encounter difficulties in their own lives. Your sorrow will not be in vain if you are able to lead one other person to the comforting arms of the Good Shepherd.

God does not comfort us to make us comfortable
but to make us comforters.

JOHN HENRY JOWETT

God often comforts us, not by changing
the circumstances of our lives,
but by changing our attitude toward them.

S. H. B. MASTERMAN

There is no pit so deep but He is not deeper still.

CORRIE TEN BOOM

In Christ the heart of the Father is revealed,
the higher comfort there cannot be than
to rest in the Father's heart.

ANDREW MURRAY

Let your lovingkindness comfort me,
just as you promised.

PSALM 119:76 TLB

GENEROSITY

They gave in a way we did not expect:
They first gave themselves to the Lord and to us.
This is what God wants.

2 CORINTHIANS 8:5 NCV

The call to be generous can be frustrating for many people. "It's easy to be generous when you have lots of money," you may say, "but I'm struggling just to make ends meet."

The apostle Paul reveals the secret to Christian generosity. He says of the Macedonian churches, "They first gave themselves to the Lord and to us." True generosity is knowing your strengths and being willing to share them. It is giving of yourself—your time, talents, energy—rather than just your money. Give your heart to those in need. Then giving your money will be guided by the spirit of generosity.

For the Macedonian Christians, giving was not
a chore but a challenge, not a burden
but a blessing. Giving was not something
to be avoided, but a privilege to be desired.

GEORGE SWEETING

Not what we give, but what we share,
For the gift without the giver is bare.

JAMES RUSSELL LOWELL

I do not believe one can settle how much we
ought to give. I am afraid the only safe rule is
to give more than we can spare.

C. S. LEWIS

The Dead Sea is the dead sea, because
it continually receives and never gives.

AUTHOR UNKNOWN

A generous person will be enriched.

PROVERBS 11:25 NRSV

God's Forgiveness

If You, LORD, should mark iniquities, O Lord,
who could stand? But there is forgiveness with You,
that You may be feared.

PSALM 130:3–4

God's forgiveness is so great that some preachers seem hesitant to speak of its fullness and immensity for fear people might sin more freely! It doesn't work that way, however. Jesus said the one who is forgiven much loves much, and if you love God, you will want to obey Him.

You may feel there are things you have done that could not possibly be forgiven. But you would be wrong. Christ died to pay for your sins, and His was the perfect sacrifice—the debt of sin paid once and forever. There is nothing you could have done that would be so terrible His sacrifice will not cover it. Turn your heart to the Lord, and discover the boundless forgiveness of God.

God has a big eraser.

BILLY ZEOLI

I believe that the chronic unhappiness of
most Christians may be attributed to a gnawing
uneasiness lest God has not fully forgiven them,
or the fear that He expects as the price of
His forgiveness some sort of emotional penance,
which they have not furnished.

A. W. TOZER

God pardons like a mother, who kisses
the offense into everlasting forgiveness.

HENRY WARD BEECHER

Nothing in this low and ruined world bears
the meek impress of the Son of God
so surely as forgiveness.

ALICE CARY

If we confess our sins, he will forgive our sins.
We can trust God. He does what is right.
He will make us clean from all the wrongs
we have done.

1 JOHN 1:9 NCV

COMMITMENT

Many proclaim themselves loyal,
but who can find one worthy of trust?

Commitment is the key to the Christian life. No man can have joy and peace until he has surrendered all to Jesus Christ.

Are you fully committed? You can find out by asking yourself a few questions:

If God asked me to give up my greatest pleasure, would I do it? If He asked me to face my greatest fear, would I do it? If He asked me to do something embarrassing, costly, or difficult, would I do it?

If you can answer yes to these questions, you need not worry about your commitment. If you cannot answer yes, pray God will change your heart—and expect Him to test your decision.

Take my life, and let it be consecrated,
Lord, to thee.

FRANCES RIDLEY HAVERGAL

God calls us to be 100 percent committed. ...
Dante said, "The hottest places in hell
are reserved for those who in times of great moral
crisis maintain their neutrality."

GEORGE SWEETING

Wherever you are, be all there.
Live to the hilt every situation
you believe to be the will of God.

JIM ELLIOT

Unless commitment is made,
there are only promises and hope ...
but no plans.

PETER DRUCKER

LORD, *who may dwell in your sanctuary?*
Who may live on your holy hill?
He ... who keeps his oath even when it hurts.

PSALM 15:1, 4 NIV

GOD'S GOODNESS

Oh, taste and see that the LORD is good;
blessed is the man who trusts in Him!

PSALM 34:8

The word "goodness" may conjure up an image in your mind of a Goody Two-shoes—the kind of person who never appears to do anything wrong and looks down his nose at the smallest failure in others. But true goodness has no trace of self-righteousness. It is, in fact, an attribute of God.

Goodness is what motivates God to be so kind and caring to undeserving sinners. It is why He is so gracious in answering our prayers. It is why He looks upon us with favor and blesses us with good things. It is why He loves us so completely despite our failings. How has God been good to you?

Seek to cultivate a buoyant, joyous sense of
the crowded kindnesses of God in your daily life.

ALEXANDER MACLAREN

The Infinite Goodness has such wide arms that
it takes whatever turns to it.

DANTE ALIGHIERI

The Lord's goodness surrounds us
at every moment. I walk through it almost
with difficulty, as through thick grass and flowers.

R. W. BARBOUR

Think of how good God is! He gives us
the physical, mental, and spiritual ability
to work in his kingdom, and then
he rewards us for doing it!

ERWIN W. LUTZER

*How great is your goodness, which you have stored up
for those who fear you.*

PSALM 31:19 NIV

FRESH START

*There must be a spiritual renewal of
your thoughts and attitudes.*

EPHESIANS 4:23 NLT

When you become a child of God, you are given a fresh start—your sins are forgiven, your mistakes are behind you, and you have eternity ahead of you. Don't ever let go of that sense of newness.

The apostle Paul said when you are in Christ, you are a new creation—that's present tense! Christ's life in you is perpetually new. And that's backed up by the prophet Jeremiah who said God's mercies are new every morning. Never again allow your life to become stale and commonplace. Just as you wouldn't think of leaving the house in the morning without taking a shower, don't leave home without confessing your faults to God and walking away spiritually cleansed and refreshed.

The sense of newness is simply delicious. It makes
new the Bible, and friends, and all mankind,
and love, and spiritual things, and Sunday,
and church, and God Himself. So I've found.

TEMPLE GARDNER OF CAIRO

I have learned one important thing in my life—
how to begin again.

SAM KEEN

If you have made mistakes, even serious mistakes,
there is always another chance for you.
And … you may have a fresh start any moment
you choose, for this thing that we call "failure"
is not the falling down, but the staying down.

MARY PICKFORD

When by the Spirit of God, I understood
these words, "The just shall live by faith,"
I felt born again like a new man: I entered
through the open doors into
the very Paradise of God!

MARTIN LUTHER

You have begun to live the new life. In your new life,
you are being made new. You are becoming
like the One who made you.

COLOSSIANS 3:10 NCV

COMPASSION

The LORD is gracious and full of compassion,
slow to anger and great in mercy.

PSALM 145:8

Do you find it difficult to feel compassion for certain people? A professional athlete gets suspended for punching out a referee. A neighbor wrecks his car after driving drunk. A teenager does poorly in school simply because he won't take the time to study. It must seem to you they really don't deserve your compassion.

When you feel that way, it's good to remember you were once in the same condition. You may not have punched a referee or driven drunk, but you almost certainly behaved foolishly in some way. And yet, God looked down on you and poured out His compassion on you when you least deserved it. Be the child of your Father in heaven. Reach out to others—even if they don't deserve it.

Christianity demands a level of caring
that transcends human inclinations.

ERWIN W. LUTZER

Did you ever take a *real* trip down inside
the broken heart of a friend? To feel the sob of
the soul—the raw, red crucible of
emotional agony? Then, to sit down
with him—and silently weep?
This is the beginning of compassion.

JESS MOODY

The Christian's compassion must be like God's—
unceasing.

WILLIAM BARCLAY

A leader must have compassion.
Nehemiah was such a man. ...
Nehemiah was called to build the wall,
but first he wept over the ruins.

CHARLES R. SWINDOLL

Be kind and compassionate to one another,
forgiving each other, just as in Christ God forgave you.
EPHESIANS 4:32 NIV

DETERMINATION

Don't burn out; keep yourselves fueled and aflame.
Be alert servants of the Master, cheerfully expectant.
Don't quit in hard times; pray all the harder.

ROMANS 12:11–12 THE MESSAGE

Have you ever wondered if life is worth the trouble? After all, it seems to be filled with heartache and disappointment and frustration. Sometimes, it's just plain boring and exhausting. God understands you will sometimes feel like giving up. But He wants you to keep on going, refusing to quit until you have fulfilled the purpose for which He created you. That is determination.

God knows that every day of your life is important, worth living. One day there will be sweet rest. But for now, God is urging you to set your course and determine to see it through. And you should know He is even more determined than you could ever be to see you finish the race He's set before you.

A strong will, a settled purpose,
an invincible determination can accomplish
almost anything.

THOMAS FULLER

Lord, give me the determination
and tenacity of a weed.

MRS. LEON R. WALTERS

The difference between the impossible
and the possible lies in a person's determination.

TOMMY LASORDA

When faced with a mountain, I will not quit!
I will keep on striving until I climb over,
find a pass through, tunnel underneath ...
or simply stay and turn the mountain into
a gold mine, with God's help.

ROBERT HAROLD SCHULLER

We must not become tired of doing good. ...
We must not give up!

GALATIANS 6:9 NCV

FORGIVENESS

Jesus said, "If you forgive men their trespasses,
your heavenly Father will also forgive you.
But if you do not forgive men their trespasses,
neither will your Father forgive your trespasses."

MATTHEW 6:14–15

Someone has wronged you—again. It's happened before, and you have no reason to believe it won't happen again. Even though that person has asked for forgiveness, you wonder if he or she really deserves it.

The apostle Peter posed that very dilemma to Jesus one day. "Should I forgive as many as seven times?" he asked. Jesus' response must have startled him. "Not seven times," Jesus told him, "but seventy times seven" (Matthew 18:22).

God doesn't ask you to continue to place yourself in the path of another's hurtful acts. But He does instruct you to forgive after the fact—primarily for your own sake. Unforgiveness can only harm the one who holds it.

We are most like men when we judge.
We are most like God when we forgive.

WILLIAM ARTHUR WARD

A cartoon in the New Yorker magazine showed an exasperated father saying to his prodigal son, "This is the fourth time we've killed the fatted calf." God does that over and over in our lifetime.

BRUCE LARSON

Forgiveness is surrendering my right to hurt you for hurting me.

ARCHIBALD HART

Forgiveness is not an occasional act, it is a permanent attitude.

MARTIN LUTHER KING JR.

Be gentle and ready to forgive; never hold grudges.
Remember, the Lord forgave you,
so you must forgive others.

COLOSSIANS 3:13 TLB

GROWTH

We should no longer be children ... but,
speaking the truth in love, may grow up in
all things into Him who is the head—Christ.

EPHESIANS 4:14–15

Where there is life, there is growth. That fact certainly holds true in the physical realm. Children grow up. Trees grow tall. And in the same way, that fact applies to a life of faith. When you surrender yourself to God and become His child, a spiritual birth occurs and a spiritual baby is born. From that day forward, spiritual growth begins to take place.

If you are a new babe in the life of faith, you can ensure your spiritual growth by finding nourishment in the Word of God, learning from more mature believers, and staying close to your heavenly Father. You have chosen to become a child of God. Now, let Him help you grow strong in the life of faith.

The strongest principle of growth lies
in human choice.

GEORGE ELIOT

Man was made to grow, not stop.

ROBERT BROWNING

Before there can be spiritual growth,
there must be spiritual life.

GEORGE SWEETING

Progress in the Christian life is exactly equal
to the growing knowledge we gain of
the Triune God in personal experience.

A. W. TOZER

See that you go on growing in the Lord,
and become strong and vigorous in the truth
you were taught.

COLOSSIANS 2:7 TLB

FINANCES

Jesus said, "Seek the kingdom of God,
and these things shall be added to you."

Luke 12:31

Jesus talked a lot about finances. Even back then, people seemed preoccupied with money and possessions. He often reminded His disciples that gold and silver are the currencies of this world, but they cannot buy the most important things of all—love, peace, joy, hope, courage, understanding, happiness, wisdom, eternal life. And that's the short list.

The truth is money is very limited. If you have trouble believing that, look at the lives of the world's wealthy. Their money cannot buy them loving relationships, stable lifestyles, or happy homes. Only God can provide those things.

Think long and hard before you invest your time and energy in the pursuit of money. Consider instead, investing in the kingdom of God.

A man's treatment of money is the most
decisive test of his character—
how he makes it and how he spends it.

James Moffatt

Money is a means, not an end—
a tool to provide people with opportunities
to hear and accept the gospel of Christ.

CHARLES STANLEY

Money has never yet made anyone rich.

SENECA

Money is an instrument that can buy you
everything but happiness and pay your fare
to every place but heaven.

AUTHOR UNKNOWN

Keep your lives free from the love of money.
And be satisfied with what you have. God has said,
"I will never leave you; I will never forget you."

HEBREWS 13:5 NCV

CONFIDENCE

*The LORD, He is the One who goes before you.
He will be with you, He will not leave you nor
forsake you; do not fear nor be dismayed.*

DEUTERONOMY 31:8

Confidence is a positive attitude toward the future, an assurance that whatever tomorrow brings, you can meet its challenges. With that in mind, Christians should be the most confident people in the world. As a believer, you have the privilege of serving the God who holds the future in His hands.

Not one thing that happens to you surprises God or catches Him off guard. He has promised to see you through every trial, hardship, heartbreak, and disappointment. You can step into the future with confidence, knowing that the God who knows all and sees all, has already paved the way before you, and will be at your side to your journey's end.

Confidence in the natural world is self-reliance, in the spiritual world it is God-reliance.

OSWALD CHAMBERS

They can conquer who believe they can.

JOHN DRYDEN

When once a saint puts his confidence in
the election of God, no tribulation
or affliction can ever touch that confidence.

OSWALD CHAMBERS

Our confidence in Christ ... awakens us,
urges us on, and makes us active in living
righteous lives and doing good.
There is no self-confidence to compare with this.

ULRICH ZWINGLI

You have been my hope, O Sovereign LORD,
my confidence since my youth.

PSALM 71:5 NIV

ENCOURAGEMENT

Encourage each other to build each other up,
just as you are already doing.

1 THESSALONIANS 5:11 TLB

The root of the word "encouragement" means to "put courage into." What a beautiful picture of one person standing beside another saying, "Take courage!" God has given you the ability to be that person to others. Ask Him to show you those who could use a kind word, an uplifting thought, a simple prayer. They could be strangers on the street or members of your own family.

Your encouragement may help someone walk when he or she might have stumbled. You might help someone stand firm instead of giving in. And encouraging others has yet another benefit. Those around you are strengthened so they can offer you an encouraging word when you need one.

I think many Christians are "dying on the vine" for lack of encouragement from other believers.

CHARLES R. SWINDOLL

Many a time a word of praise or thanks or appreciation or cheer has kept a man on his feet. Blessed is the man who speaks such a word.

WILLIAM BARCLAY

Correction does much, but encouragement does more. Encouragement after censure is as the sun after a shower.

JOHANN WOLFGANG VON GOETHE

Encouragement is oxygen to the soul.

GEORGE M. ADAMS

If one has the gift of encouraging others,
he should encourage.

ROMANS 12:8 NCV

FAITH

The Lord said, "If you have faith as a mustard seed,
you can say to this mulberry tree,
'Be pulled up by the roots and be planted in the sea,'
and it would obey you."

Some people think they should store up their faith to be ready for an emergency. That makes about as much sense as an athlete staying in bed for a week to conserve his strength for the big game. Faith is like a muscle. It won't become strong unless you exercise it.

Be bold; step out in faith and give your spiritual muscles a good workout on a regular basis. Attempt great things for God, trusting in His provision. It won't be long before you will feel yourself growing stronger, better able to tackle the challenges in your life with faith and power.

A faith that hasn't been tested can't be trusted.

ADRIAN ROGERS

Attempt something so impossible that
unless God is in it, it's doomed to failure.

JOHN HAGGAI

Faith is a living, daring confidence in God's grace,
so sure and certain that a man could stake
his life on it a thousand times.

MARTIN LUTHER

Faith and obedience are bound up in the same
bundle; he that obeys God trusts God;
and he that trusts God obeys God.
He that is without faith is without works,
and he that is without works is without faith.

CHARLES HADDON SPURGEON

*Dear brothers, giving thanks to God for you is not
only the right thing to do, but it is our duty
to God because of the really wonderful way
your faith has grown.*

1 THESSALONIANS 1:3 TLB

FAMILY

*Be an example to the believers in word, in conduct,
in love, in spirit, in faith, in purity.*

1 TIMOTHY 4:12

As a Christian man, God has called you to be a spiritual leader in your home. That's an awesome responsibility and one God is eager to help you fulfill.

First of all, it means you need to set an example of godly character. That doesn't mean God expects you to be perfect. It simply means He wants you to do your best by taking advantage of the resources He's given you: reading the Bible, spending time in prayer, being willing to do the right thing.

As your family sees your effort to walk in godly character, they will be more willing to follow your godly lead. Will you step up to the plate—for your family's sake?

A man ought to live so that everybody knows
he is a Christian ... and most of all,
his family ought to know.

DWIGHT L. MOODY

A family is a place where principles
are hammered and honed on
the anvil of everyday living.

CHARLES R. SWINDOLL

There is never much trouble in any family
where the children hope someday
to resemble their parents.

WILLIAM LYON PHELPS

I believe the family was established long before
the church, and my duty is to my family first.
I am not to neglect my family.

DWIGHT L. MOODY

A leader must be well-thought-of, committed to his
wife, cool and collected, accessible, and hospitable. ...
He must handle his own affairs well, attentive to
his own children and having their respect.

1 TIMOTHY 3:2–4 THE MESSAGE

COURAGE

Behave courageously, and the LORD
will be with the good.

2 CHRONICLES 19:11

Courage is probably not something you think of as being displayed in everyday life. It is a word that seems to be reserved mostly for war heroes or characters in a movie. But courage is more common than you might think.

The dictionary defines "courage" as the ability to face something dangerous, difficult, or painful and deal with it. You have probably done that many times without realizing you were being brave. Perhaps you have sat by the bed of a dying friend, faced a negative pattern in your life, or forgiven an erring spouse. All of those things required courage.

God knows it would be easier to run and hide than to deal courageously with some of the situations life sends your way. He's proud of you.

Courage is the first of human qualities because it is the quality that guarantees all others.

WINSTON CHURCHILL

The courage of life is often a less dramatic
spectacle than the courage of a final moment;
but it is no less a magnificent mixture of
triumph and tragedy.

JOHN F. KENNEDY

I would define true courage to be
a perfect sensibility of the measure of danger,
and a mental willingness to endure it.

GENERAL W. T. SHERMAN

The Bible is a first-hand story of goose-bump
courage in very ordinary people who were
invaded by the living God.

TIM HANSEL

Be strong! Be courageous! Do not be afraid of them!
For the Lord your God will be with you.
He will neither fail you nor forsake you.

DEUTERONOMY 31:6 TLB

FAITHFULNESS

*Jesus said, "Be faithful until death,
and I will give you the crown of life."*

REVELATION 2:10

Eugene Peterson says faithfulness is "a long obedience in the same direction." What a wonderful insight. Faithfulness is a virtue that can only be proven over time. It's not about who's there at the beginning, but who is still there at the end. When others go, will you stay? When others quit, will you hang on? That's the crux of faithfulness.

God has promised to be with you through every circumstance of your life—good and bad. He promises never to leave you nor forsake you. He has pledged His faithfulness. Will you be faithful to Him? Will you choose to trust Him when times are tough? Let God know He can count on you.

I do not pray for success; I ask for faithfulness.

MOTHER TERESA

We know that our rewards depend not on
the job itself but on the faithfulness
with which we serve God.

JOHN PAUL I

Faithfulness in little things is a big thing.

SAINT JOHN CHRYSOSTOM

He does most in God's great world
who does his best in his own little world.

THOMAS JEFFERSON

Do not let loyalty and faithfulness forsake you;
bind them around your neck,
write them on the tablet of your heart.

PROVERBS 3:3 NRSV

THANKFULNESS

In everything give thanks; for this is the will of God in Christ Jesus for you.

1 THESSALONIANS 5:18

How do you feel when you go out of your way for someone and that person takes the time to say "thank you"? God also likes to hear you acknowledge all the good things He's done for you.

Even if your life has been way less than perfect, you will be able to find plenty of things to be grateful to God for—a roof over your head, a sky filled with stars, the love of family and friends, a special talent or skill, His unwavering presence in your life. The wonderful thing is the more you express your thankfulness, the more He pours out His blessings on your life.

Why hesitate? Give Him your thanks right now!

Thou has given so much to me. ...
Give me one thing more—a grateful heart.

GEORGE HERBERT

Thankfulness is a soil in which pride
does not easily grow.

MICHAEL RAMSAY

Gratitude to God makes even a temporal
blessing a taste of heaven.

WILLIAM ROMAINE

Gratitude is not only the memory but
the homage of the heart—rendered to God
for his goodness.

NATHANIEL PARKER WILLIS

Give thanks to the LORD, for he is good;
his love endures forever.

PSALM 107:1 NIV

TOPICAL INDEX

Additional copies of this book
and other titles from ELM HILL PRESS
are available from your local bookstore.

Other titles in this series:

God's Daily Answer
God's Daily Answer for Teachers
God's Daily Answer for Women
God's Daily Answer for Graduates
God's Daily Answer for Mothers
God's Daily Answer Devotional